RED MEAT GOLD

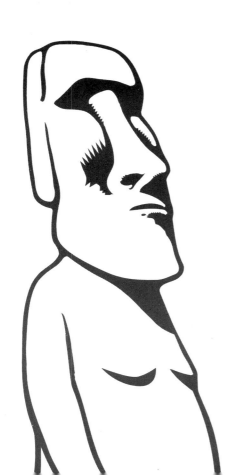

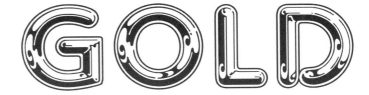

Also by Max Cannon

a collection of **RED MEAT** cartoons

the second collection of **RED MEAT** cartoons

RED MEAT

GOLD

the third collection of RED MEAT cartoons

from the secret files of Max Cannon

with a foreword by Stephen Thompson, Editor, *The Onion A.V. Club*

St. Martin's
Griffin
New York

For information, address St. Martin's Press, 175 Fifth Avenue, New York, N.Y. 10010.

www.stmartins.com

RED MEAT is available for weekly newspaper syndication. For information and rates email: meatbiz@redmeat.com, or write to: P.O. Box 41115, Tucson, Arizona 85717

For an online archive of RED MEAT strips, news, and a selection of quality American-made merchandise and apparel, please visit the official RED MEAT web site at www.redmeat.com

ISBN 0-312-33014-6
EAN 978-0312-33014-9

First Edition: April 2005

10 9 8 7 6 5 4 3 2 1

FOREWORD by Stephen Thompson, Editor, *The Onion A.V. Club*

At this point, it's standard operating procedure to rail against the homogeneity and unnerving jokelessness of the American comics page. In fact, complaining about it has become so trite that it's tempting to let the pendulum swing the other way—to openly embrace Ziggy, B.C., and the sundry strips whose creators continue to churn out surreally pointless panels despite having died in 1966. But not even kitsch appreciation can make much of the modern comics page engaging, readable, or relevant.

Against this depressing backdrop, *The Onion* began running Max Cannon's RED MEAT in the fall of 1993. At that time, the four-year-old comic strip's playful juxtaposition of stylized icons and sick humor made it a natural candidate for a cult following—and a perfect fit for *The Onion's* own sensibility, in which humor and horror can be inseparable, if not indistinguishable. More than ten years later, Max's work has never been more widely distributed, finding a huge audience online, in about eighty-five weekly newspapers, and, of course, in *The Onion,* where he'll have a home until the precise moment when one of us starts to suck beyond recognition.

Anyone can do gross-out gags, but RED MEAT showcases a rare ability to transform stomach-churning subject matter—the body's wriggling entrails and caustic leavings, eviscerated or otherwise misused animals, inhuman horrors visited upon children and their long-suffering pets—into sublime poetry. As striking as his visuals are, Max's words are what sear indelible images into readers' imaginations.

Naturally, this cavalcade of grotesquerie is big with European media types, who assume that any fucked-up art to emerge from the U.S. must be attempting to expose the nation's rotting underbelly. But RED MEAT isn't really about the rotting underbelly of America, or suburbia, or the comics page, but about the rotting underbelly of the human mind. It's about the strange, twisted power of mere words—and how, when strung together in just the right order, they can be gorier than any crime-scene photo.

The ever-changing phrases atop each weekly installment of RED MEAT bear this out beautifully, but best of them all is the characteristically alliterative mission statement buried somewhere in this book: "Firmly fastened to the milk sac of misanthropy." When Max Cannon himself goes the way of young Karen's many ill-fated puppies, he's already dictated his own epitaph.

—**Stephen Thompson**

RED MEAT
the whacky world of two-by-fours
from the secret files of
Max Cannon
The other night I was roller skating with my girlfriend, and she's not a very good skater. Anyways, she fell and split her scalp open.
The whole time, I couldn't help noticing that she'd look pretty good as a redhead.

RED MEAT
the white-hot cure for sticky valves
from the secret files of
max cannon
Dad...I'm going out to the lobby for a little while.
What's the matter...don't like the movie?
The movie was over twenty minutes ago.
Oh...you're right. Is there any bourbon left?
No. The usher took it after the second time we mooned the projectionist.

RED MEAT
butterfly appliqués on the sliding glass door of doom
from the secret files of Max Cannon
Hey Baby, I think you better take a look at these corn flakes. It looks to me like they're completely infested with worms and beetles.
Those aren't corn flakes...that's muesli. It's a Swiss cereal, with all kinds of good things in it. It'll give you some good fiber.
Tell you what, honey...how about you make me some delicious, colon-clogging, American cream of wheat, and I'll make sure to eat a big handful of earwigs on my way to work.
Don't mess with me today, Don.

RED MEAT
itch-fighting cortex ointment
from the secret files of
Max Cannon
Good morning, Dan. Not working today?
My manager gave me a week off.
He strongly recommended I use the time to enter a "substance treatment" program.
I see.
Well, as your unofficial medical advisor, I recommend that I immediately treat you to a substance known as "ice-cold beer."
I'm feeling better already.

RED MEAT

the doleful mewling of
freshly-weened wussies

from the secret files of
MAX Cannon

One winter, while my brother and I were out hiking, we found a dead clown under a pile of old tarpaper. We thought it might be the same dead clown we'd found the summer before, but it was so shriveled up, we couldn't tell.

Then I remembered that the clown we found in the summer had a tattoo of a rose on his left arm. When I lifted up the arm to look, it snapped off like an old dried-up tree branch.

We broke off the other arm and both of the legs and stacked them off to the side. Then we found a piece of cardboard and made a sign that said: "BUILD YOUR OWN CLOWN."

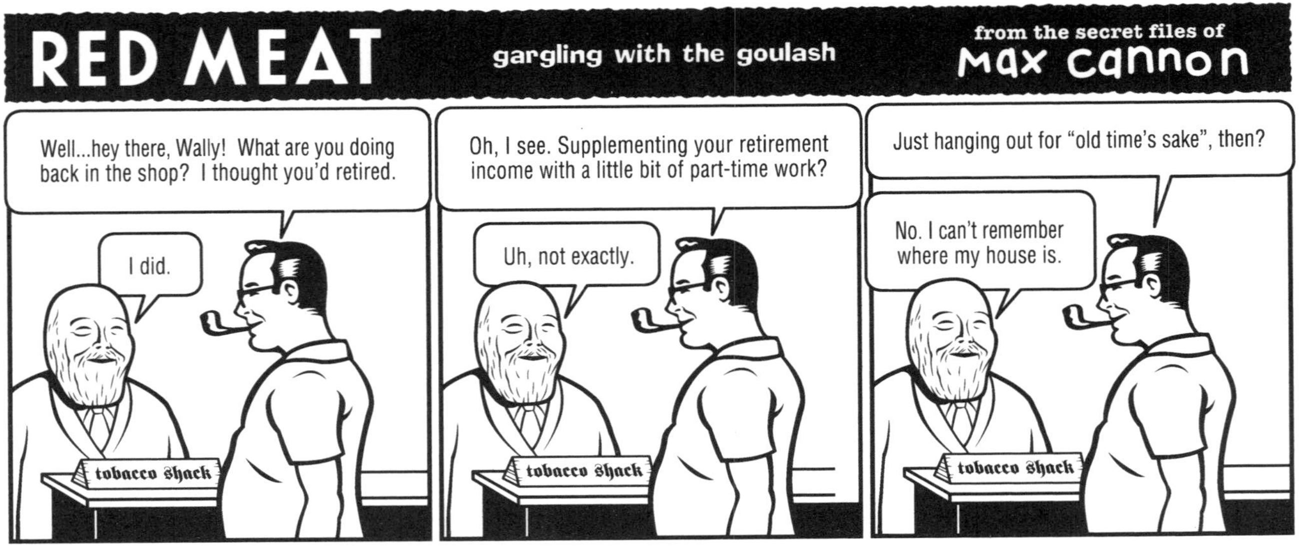
RED MEAT
gargling with the goulash
from the secret files of
Max Cannon
Well...hey there, Wally! What are you doing back in the shop? I thought you'd retired.
I did.
tobacco shack
Oh, I see. Supplementing your retirement income with a little bit of part-time work?
Uh, not exactly.
tobacco shack
Just hanging out for "old time's sake", then?
No. I can't remember where my house is.
tobacco shack

RED MEAT
first dibs on the last rites
from the secret files of
Max Cannon
I had to move to a new apartment recently. The old place was gettin' a little too small for me an' my cat.
You'd be surprised how much space it takes for a cheetah to ride a dirt bike.

RED MEAT

butter-side-down in the diaper bucket

from the secret files of
Max Cannon

What's the matter...not enjoying the movie?

The movie's fine. I just can't focus on anything because of that awful smell.

That's what rotten eggs smell like, Son.

They're ruining the movie, Dad.

Sorry, I had to improvise. If we'd gotten to the theater a little early, we could've scored good seats by more conventional means.

Here, put some Vap-O-Rub on your upper lip.

RED MEAT
skid marks on your skullcap
from the secret files of
max cannon
Well hello, Nick. Uh...it's a funny thing running into you like this.
Yeah...?
What I mean is, it's not very often that I have the opportunity to see my son's gym teacher naked...not to mention running laps inside of a crowded grocery store.
Tell you what, Johnson...you quit smoking your way, and I'll do it mine. Besides, I'm not naked—I'm wearing a nicotine patch.
Well what do you know...? I had no idea they made those babies in a "thong" style.

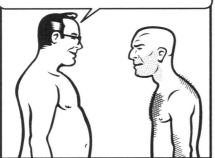

RED MEAT
wrinkled knee on the leotards of lethargy
from the secret files of Max Cannon
I must admit, Nick...these new "thong-style" nicotine patches really work. I have no urge to smoke, plus I'm also cool and comfortable.
Well, Johnson...I'm glad it's working out, but you might want to read the instructions.
I'm pretty sure the triangular part goes on your front side.
Hmm...I don't think so. That looks like it might chafe a bit.

RED MEAT
nourishing nuggets of nether nougat
from the secret files of
Max Cannon
Gaze upon me...
If I wouldn't look when it was screamin,'
what makes it think I'm gonna look now?

RED MEAT
glistening suction cups on the headboard of hebetude
from the secret files of max cannon
I'm very excited for you, Son. Dropping you off at camp brings back quite a few fond memories of my first time at summer camp.
Really?
Oh sure. For instance, on my first night the other guys in my cabin secretly put a black widow in my bunk, and the darn thing laid an egg sac under my scalp while I was asleep.
What happened?
One week later, I was the proud mother of three hundred babies. But that was kid stuff compared to the time I got stuffed into the latrine. They couldn't find me for two days.
I'm just gonna kill myself now.
Buck up, son. That's what the counselors are here for.

RED MEAT
the squirting squids of squalor
from the secret files of
max cannon
Say...what's the matter Karen? You look like you're about to start crying.
What are you talking about, Milkman Dan? I'm not about to cry.
That's funny...
Dan
If an intoxicated adult in a three-quarter ton milk delivery vehicle just carelessly ran over a box of my dolls, I'd start crying.
So would I, but those weren't dolls in there... the Hell's Angels were givin' away free puppies.
Dan
Whoops.
Dan

RED MEAT
the crinkley caress of crenulated crevice clips
from the secret files of
max cannon
Hey, Johnson...I need to borrow your electric pine cone trimmer for awhile.
Yeah, hold on...I'll go get it.
Damn, Ted...I was just joking around with you. Why the hell would anybody have an electric pine cone trimmer?
I know what you mean, Don. The old gas-powered "Pine Weasel P-391" gave you vastly superior lateral cone-shaping control.

RED MEAT

comedy's cauterized stump

from the secret files of **Max Cannon**

There's this restaurant that I go to every mornin' for breakfast, because I kinda like this one pretty waitress that works there.

This mornin' she tells me: "Don't come in here no more, Earl...because you're always starin' at me an' it gives me the creeps."

If I'd'a known she was like that, I never would've carved her name in my chest.

RED MEAT
retro-fitting for the unwitting
from the secret files of
Max Cannon
Dad...don't you think that shirt is a little bit too small for you?
This is a "babydoll", son. All of the kids are wearing them.
Oh, I get it. You're trying to get out of going to the father-son picnic with me.
Come on now, son...
What makes you think I'm trying to get out of going to the picnic with you?
Well...for starters, Dad, you usually don't wear teal-colored hot pants.
If it makes you feel better I'll go put my velour chaps on over them.

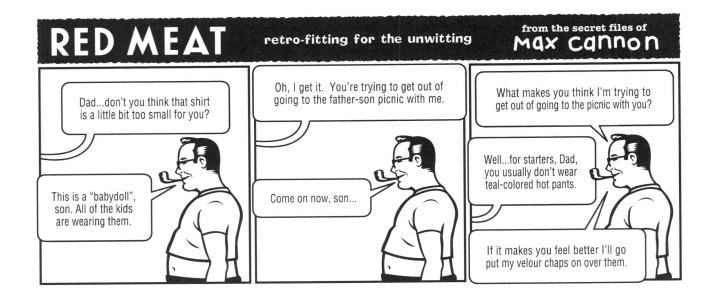

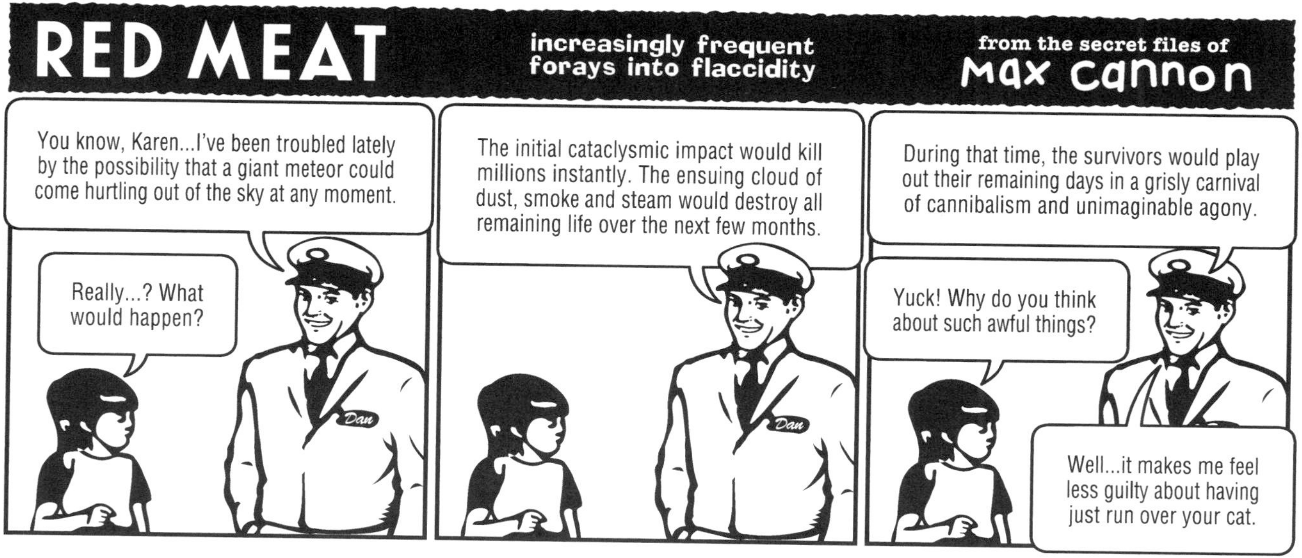
RED MEAT
increasingly frequent forays into flaccidity
from the secret files of
max cannon
You know, Karen...I've been troubled lately by the possibility that a giant meteor could come hurtling out of the sky at any moment.
Really...? What would happen?
Dan
The initial cataclysmic impact would kill millions instantly. The ensuing cloud of dust, smoke and steam would destroy all remaining life over the next few months.
Dan
During that time, the survivors would play out their remaining days in a grisly carnival of cannibalism and unimaginable agony.
Yuck! Why do you think about such awful things?
Well...it makes me feel less guilty about having just run over your cat.

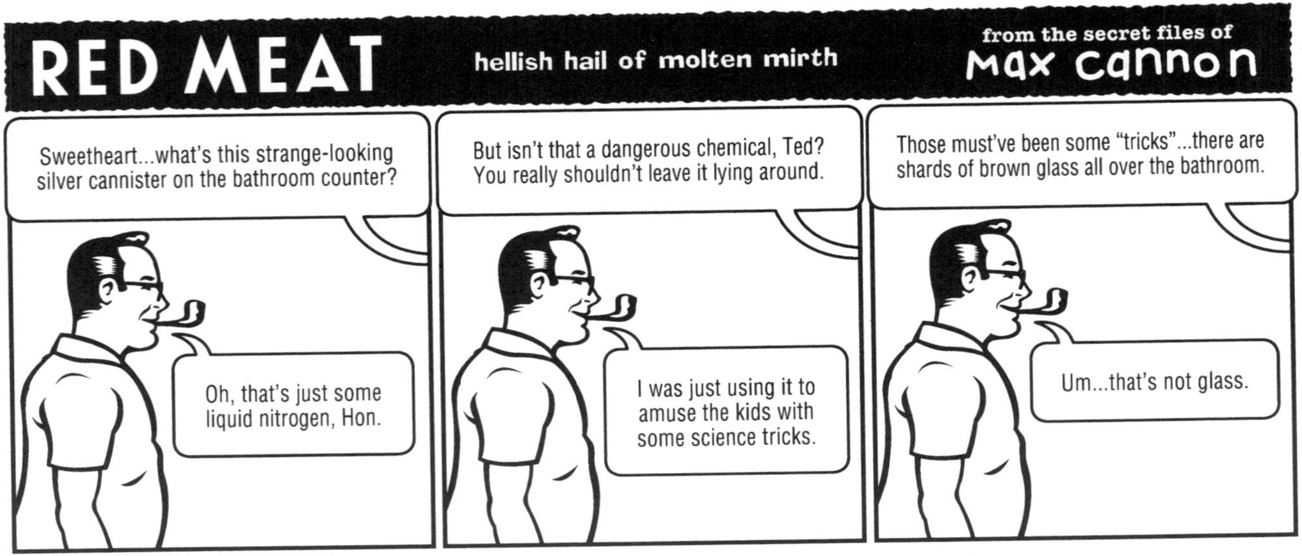
RED MEAT
hellish hail of molten mirth
from the secret files of
Max Cannon
Sweetheart...what's this strange-looking silver cannister on the bathroom counter?
Oh, that's just some liquid nitrogen, Hon.
But isn't that a dangerous chemical, Ted? You really shouldn't leave it lying around.
I was just using it to amuse the kids with some science tricks.
Those must've been some "tricks"...there are shards of brown glass all over the bathroom.
Um...that's not glass.

RED MEAT

perdition's pogo stick

from the secret files of
Max Cannon

Before you make any derogatory remarks about my costume, Karen, I think you should know you're looking at the new "McMoo the Anti-Drug Cow" for your school district.

Ha! Milkman Dan playing McMoo...? That's a big laugh!

HEY!!

SQUIRT!

Sorry about that, Karen. For a moment there, I thought you might be on drugs.

25

RED MEAT
the mellifluous milk of monotony
from the secret files of
max cannon
Hmm...mouth is dry, can't feel my tongue, blurred vision, hands and legs are numb, I just went to the bathroom in my pants, and now I'm seeing lightning bolts coming out of my cardigan buttons.
ZZZAK!
No wonder you're not supposed to drink furniture polish.

RED MEAT the rippling rugae of recompense from the secret files of Max Cannon

Ted, Sweetheart...why are you hanging upside down in that metal tube?

I'm trying a little gravity experiment, Hon. I just swallowed a half pound of quarters... and I want to see which direction they go.

CHA-CHINK!
CHA-CHINK!
CHA-CHINK!

Hmm. Another great moment in science.

No dice, Honey...those were just the nickels I ate yesterday. It's going to be another eight hours before we have "quarter data".

27

RED MEAT
tedium's oaken tent pole
from the secret files of
max cannon
It was late in the fall when my dad told us that we couldn't keep that shriveled dead clown in his shed any longer. My brother and I didn't have the heart to simply throw it away...it had brought us such joy since the day we found it.
So we bought a ladies' wig at the second-hand store and spray painted it red. We put the wig on the clown and took him downtown to the McDonald's and left him in one of the booths.
FUN
When my dad read about it in the paper the next day, he put us on restriction for a whole month. We thought it was worth it, though... that dead clown was the funniest thing ever.
COUNTY MORGUE
D.O.A.
#1704 JOHN DOE

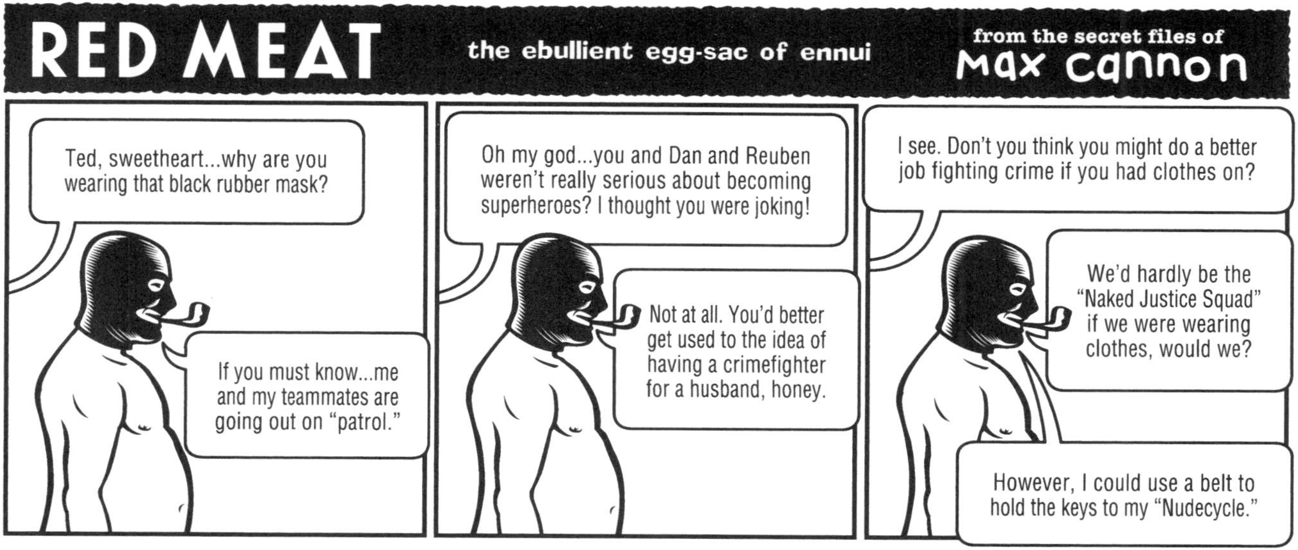

RED MEAT
the ebullient egg-sac of ennui
from the secret files of
max cannon
Ted, sweetheart...why are you wearing that black rubber mask?
If you must know...me and my teammates are going out on "patrol."
Oh my god...you and Dan and Reuben weren't really serious about becoming superheroes? I thought you were joking!
Not at all. You'd better get used to the idea of having a crimefighter for a husband, honey.
I see. Don't you think you might do a better job fighting crime if you had clothes on?
We'd hardly be the "Naked Justice Squad" if we were wearing clothes, would we?
However, I could use a belt to hold the keys to my "Nudecycle."

RED MEAT
mysterious mound on your mantelpiece
from the secret files of
Max Cannon
Good Lord, Milkman Dan...you're covered in blood! Should I go call the paramedics?
Dan
No need, Father...I'm perfectly fine. I was just testing out my new turbo propellor-driven milk delivery vehicle.
Dan
They certainly do put those city bus stops close to the street, don't they?
Dan

RED MEAT
the buckling beams of your hopes and dreams
from the secret files of
max cannon
You weren't kidding, Ted...cigars do have a natural laxative effect. But I still don't think I can do it.
Sure you can. Give it try.
≡ Gnngh ≡ Nope. Not gonna happen.
Maybe I should just sign my letter of resignation with a pen, instead.
Come on...at least do your initials.

RED MEAT that solid waste aftertaste from the secret files of **Max Cannon**

Ted...did you put new headlights on the station wagon since I last drove it?

Sure did, Honey. Those babies are 10,000 watt halogen "Pathstalkers." Intense...aren't they?

Intense...?! I drove over to pick up the boys in front of the school, and I could see their bones and organs right through their skin!

Don't worry, Sweetheart. Seeing that kind of thing will just take some getting used to.

Well I might, Ted...if the kids still had skin.

Look at it this way... you won't have to buy Halloween costumes for anybody this year.

32

RED MEAT

sandpaper backrub

from the secret files of
Max Cannon

Oh Lord, I feel that many of my flock have strayed from your word. What can I do to lead them back into the fold?

I find that most folks listen better if you use a funny hand puppet. Here...borrow mine.

Hey, wait...come back, guy. I was only kidding around.

RED MEAT
two-and-a-half-inch denture screws
from the secret files of
Max Cannon
Whoo-ee, betty! If this here busted fencepost is a'whut I think it is...I 'spect I'll be spendin' rest'a the gol'dang day roundin' up chickens.
I reckon them crazy birds must'a been pokin' around in that bag'a experimental livestock feed whut the county agent done left here t'other day.
Shoot...if they ate as much of the dad-blamed stuff as me'n'Lyle did, they're prob'ly over to the barn takin' turns on that poor ol' heifer, too.

RED MEAT

dutch rub on your nether lands

from the secret files of
Max Cannon

Good god, Nick...you look like hell. Did you get in a fight or something?

Yeah, sort of.

Couple'a punks jumped me over in the park. We went around pretty good for awhile, 'til I started throwing up blood.

That could be serious. We'd better get you to a hospital.

Relax, Johnson...it wasn't my blood.

I see. Then that rib sticking out of your hip isn't yours, either?

RED MEAT
hellhole swan dive
from the secret files of
max cannon
I watched this movie about Ben Hur on the TV last night. It reminded me about when I was a kid an' I use'ta like to play "gladiator."
I used a big cooking pot for a helmet, an' a toilet plunger for a sword, an' me and the neighbor kids used to have these wars.
Man...it takes a lot of work to kill a kid with a plunger.

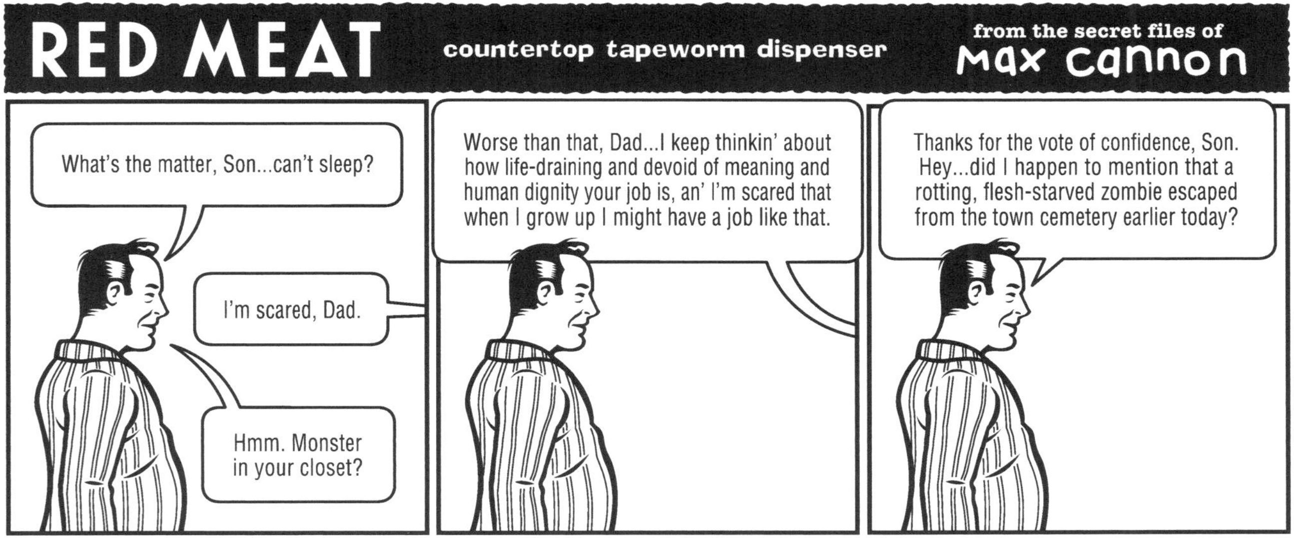
RED MEAT
countertop tapeworm dispenser
from the secret files of
Max Cannon
What's the matter, Son...can't sleep?
I'm scared, Dad.
Hmm. Monster in your closet?
Worse than that, Dad...I keep thinkin' about how life-draining and devoid of meaning and human dignity your job is, an' I'm scared that when I grow up I might have a job like that.
Thanks for the vote of confidence, Son. Hey...did I happen to mention that a rotting, flesh-starved zombie escaped from the town cemetery earlier today?

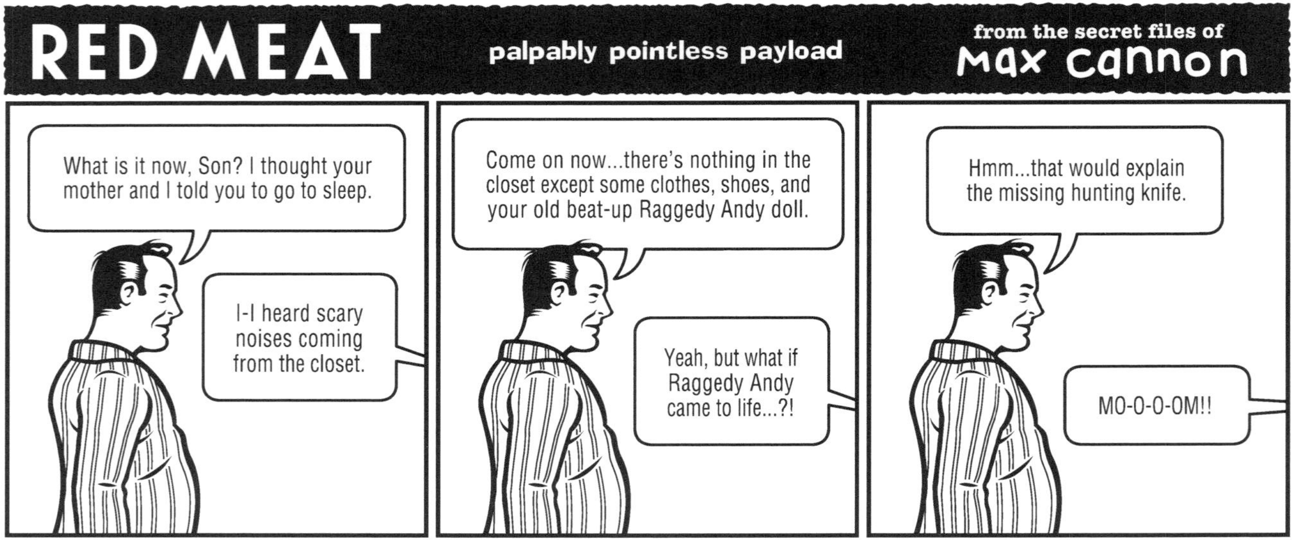
RED MEAT
palpably pointless payload
from the secret files of
Max Cannon
What is it now, Son? I thought your mother and I told you to go to sleep.
I-I heard scary noises coming from the closet.
Come on now...there's nothing in the closet except some clothes, shoes, and your old beat-up Raggedy Andy doll.
Yeah, but what if Raggedy Andy came to life...?!
Hmm...that would explain the missing hunting knife.
MO-O-O-OM!!

RED MEAT

vapo-rub in your margarine tub

from the secret files of
Max Cannon

Hey Ted, remember that night when we first met our wives back in nineteen seventy-six?

How could I forget?

Okay, my main man...I'm gonna make it with Cindy and you get it on with Sheila.

What it is. Sheila is a stone-cold solid fox.

Was that dance club really dark...or did Sheila have a mustache back then, too?

Geez, Don...seemed like in those days everybody had facial hair.

RED MEAT
the mouldering mounds of mirth
from the secret files of
max cannon
I'm doin' a little artistic exercise today, so I'm stayin' in this closet 'til I can come up with a decent idea for the story I'm writin'.
So far it's a toss-up between a story about a guy who has to go to the bathroom real bad, and one about a guy who's real hungry.

RED MEAT
heart-shaped patch on the quilt of inappropriateness
from the secret files of max cannon
You know, Karen, part of my job as "McMoo the anti-drug cow" is to make sure kids eat right and drink lots of milk. How'd you like a refill on that refreshing glass of cold milk?
Okay...I guess so.
OWW!! That's hot coffee!
SQUIRT!
Coffee? Hmmh...I could swear I filled those reservoirs up with urine earlier.

RED MEAT
the redolent remnants of roughage
from the secret files of
Max Cannon
Enjoying the movie, Son?
Uh, why are you asking me that?
Well, you seem a bit bored, but I don't get it. I mean, this movie has it all: gunfire, chases, naked ladies, alien space ships, explosions...
Uh-huh.
Better let me have some of that cough syrup, Dad...because we're still sittin' in the car in the theater parking lot.

RED MEAT

bubbling bilge pump bisque

from the secret files of
Max cannon

Hey, Ted...I'm a little short on rent this month. Would you happen to have any odd jobs that I could do for some cash?

Good question, Johnny...let me think.

You know...I'd happily pay you four dollars to thrash around on a vinyl tarp covered in melted butter while I throw oranges at you.

Gosh...I don't know about that.

Well, it's obvious to me that you're not too interested in doing "odd" jobs. How about some yard work or something?

Okay.

Great. Three dollars to rake the yard, and I still get to throw the oranges.

RED MEAT

halfheartedly flung onto the fun heap

from the secret files of
Max Cannon

Whoo man...I tell you what. Ain't nothin' sweet as the late afternoon a'settin' over them prairie hills, paintin' them shadows all purple-color.

Hells bells...it's like the good lord done take a bucket'a liquid gold an' flung it all over the top of ever'thing in creation. It's dad-blamed purty.

'Course, I could do without them lime-colored twinklies a'flyin' round ever'where —not only're they ugly, but they're makin' the horses melt.

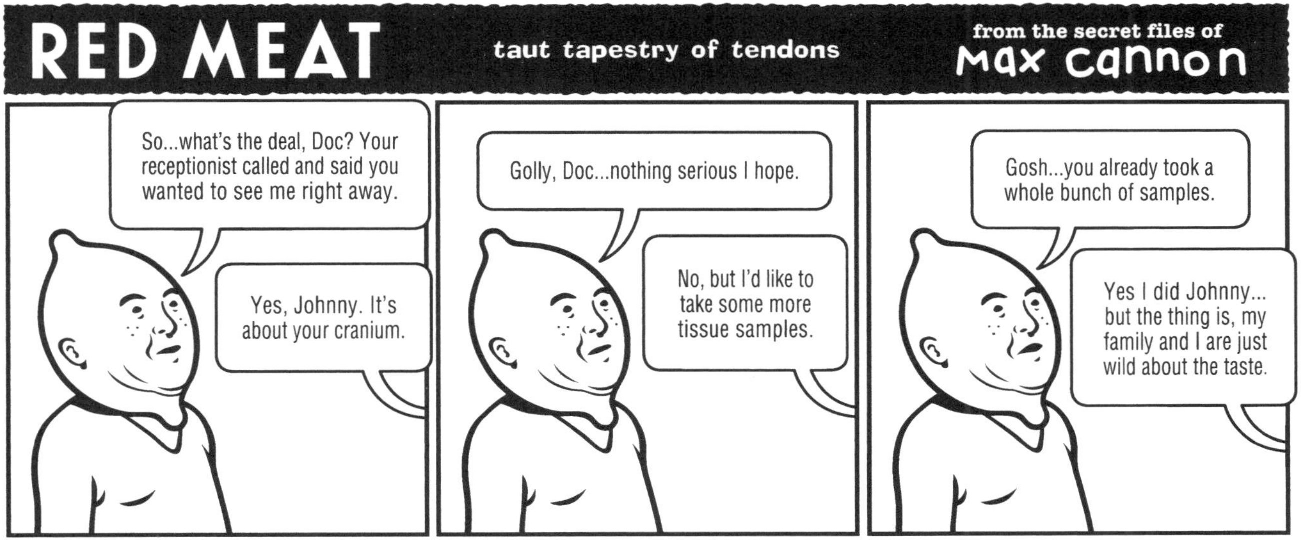
RED MEAT
taut tapestry of tendons
from the secret files of
Max Cannon
So...what's the deal, Doc? Your receptionist called and said you wanted to see me right away.
Yes, Johnny. It's about your cranium.
Golly, Doc...nothing serious I hope.
No, but I'd like to take some more tissue samples.
Gosh...you already took a whole bunch of samples.
Yes I did Johnny... but the thing is, my family and I are just wild about the taste.

RED MEAT

the lukewarm lather of lethargy

from the secret files of **MAX CANNON**

One of my coworkers at the dairy told me a joke at lunch today that was so hilarious it made cottage cheese shoot out my nose.

Ewww...that's gross.

Yes it is, Karen.

More disturbingly, though...I wasn't eating cottage cheese at the time.

≡ Ulp! ≡

Whoops. Sorry, Karen...I forgot you were recovering from stomach flu.

≡ R-R-RETCH! ≡

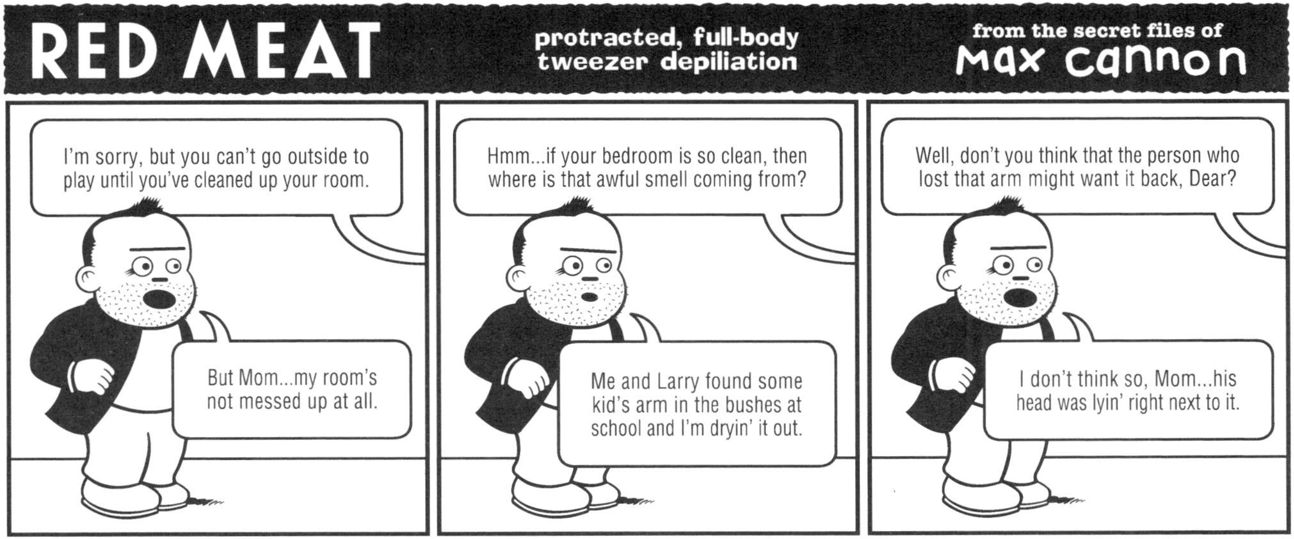
RED MEAT
protracted, full-body tweezer depiliation
from the secret files of
Max Cannon
I'm sorry, but you can't go outside to play until you've cleaned up your room.
But Mom...my room's not messed up at all.
Hmm...if your bedroom is so clean, then where is that awful smell coming from?
Me and Larry found some kid's arm in the bushes at school and I'm dryin' it out.
Well, don't you think that the person who lost that arm might want it back, Dear?
I don't think so, Mom...his head was lyin' right next to it.

RED MEAT

effluvium dunk-tank

from the secret files of
Max Cannon

I'm all done cleanin' out the rain gutters, Mrs. Rosso. Didja want me to rake the yard?

Why, sure Clyde. Perhaps after you're finished with that task you could come inside and help me rub some lotion onto my back.

No disrespect, but I don't know if I feel comfortable doin' that.

Oh...I see. Are you afraid my husband will find out?

No ma'am. It's just that I always prefer to strip, spackle and sand any old surface before applyin' a new coat of finish to it.

Ouch...sounds delicious.

I'll go git my tools, then.

48

RED MEAT
comedy's malformed twin
from the secret files of
Max Cannon
I need to use the restroom and I don't think I can make it to my home in time. Might I impose and use yours briefly?
I guess so...but robots don't need to go to the bathroom.
BLEEEEAGH!!
They do if they've drank as many tequila shooters and eaten as many jalapeño poppers as I have today.
Down the hallway... first door on the left.
HIC Muchas gracias.

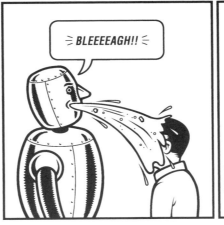

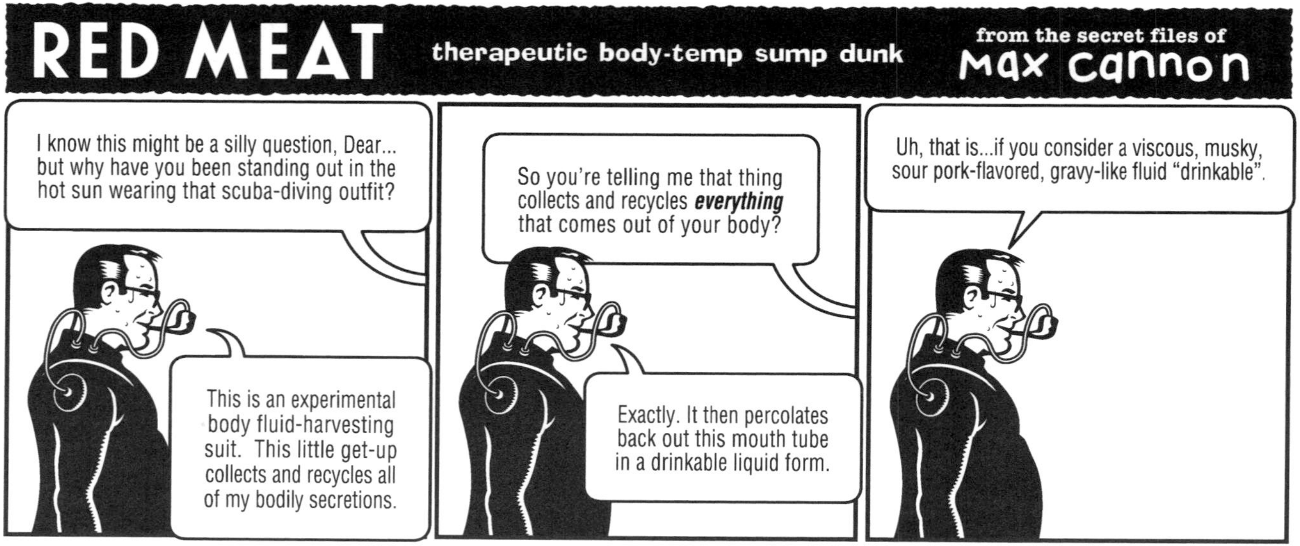

RED MEAT

therapeutic body-temp sump dunk

from the secret files of
Max Cannon

I know this might be a silly question, Dear... but why have you been standing out in the hot sun wearing that scuba-diving outfit?

This is an experimental body fluid-harvesting suit. This little get-up collects and recycles all of my bodily secretions.

So you're telling me that thing collects and recycles *everything* that comes out of your body?

Exactly. It then percolates back out this mouth tube in a drinkable liquid form.

Uh, that is...if you consider a viscous, musky, sour pork-flavored, gravy-like fluid "drinkable".

RED MEAT

eighteen wheel cross-country truculence

from the secret files of
Max Cannon

See, Karen...I told you I'd get you your own mini-version of my electrokinetically enhanced, kevlar-reinforced exo-suit.

Wow. It's really neat.

Yes, it's a thrill. But be aware that with the tremendous power contained in the "Milkman Dan Junior" suit comes great responsibility. You must promise me to always use it wisely.

I promise.

And I promise also to use my suit's power wisely. Particularly this remote switch in my pocket that delivers a painful electrical shock to the wearer of the mini-suit when I press the little red activator button like so...

I-I-I h-h-hate y-y-you m-m-Milkman d-d-Dan.

51

RED MEAT
gas-powered rainforest-wood seal club
from the secret files of
Max Cannon
Well, Karen...better get cracking. I'd like you to finish my milk delivery route on your bicycle while I take a nap. It should only take you another four or five hours.
But I have to go to school!
Dan
Jr.
Come now, little lady...you don't want me to press the remote button that activates the electro-shock unit in your exo-suit, do you?
Go ahead.
Dan
Jr.
'Cause I disconnected my unit and reversed the circuit in your suit.
I-I-I'd h-h-hug y-y-you if m-my m-muscles weren't p-painfully c-c-contracted.
Jr.

RED MEAT
hand-crocheted slipcovers for your vestigial flippers
from the secret files of Max Cannon
Good to see you, Johnny. You might have noticed that I stacked some old furniture on your porch. I figured you could use it.
I didn't see any furniture. All I saw was a big pile of sun-rotted lumber, broken beer bottles, and a bunch of rusty metal scraps.
Did I say "furniture"...? I must be going senile. I meant "spider-infested detritus."
Oh...thanks for thinking of me.

RED MEAT
trowelled-on laugh line spackle
from the secret files of
max cannon
Hi Karen...I was wondering if you had an old cardboard box that I could borrow?
What do you need it for?
Dan
I'm going to make a time machine out of it and send your puppy into the future.
Why?
Dan
Well...hopefully, in the future, they'll have the technology to reassemble all the pieces of him that I scraped out of my truck's fan housing and somehow bring them back to life.
MOM-MUH!!
Dan
Settle down...I just need a box for empty milk bottles.

RED MEAT

flat-handed cactus slap

from the secret files of
Max Cannon

Whoo-ee...just lookit that spectacular view. Ain't nothin' better'n this life...lookin' out at the sunset, smokin' and watchin' the cattle.

Sweet dang, but if this ain't the purtiest place on earth, though. This here's God's country.

The Empire State Building's observation deck is closed now, sir. Please move toward the elevator.

Hold on...I'm a'comin'.

RED MEAT
mouthful of molten muck
from the secret files of
Max cannon
My buddy told me about this old Chinese doctor that he goes to. He said this guy could give me somethin' to help my veins on my legs, 'cause they're stickin' way out.
I just figured he'd give me some kind'a root powder or homemade tea or somethin', but instead this old guy wants to stick a bunch of them sharp little acu-punchers in me.
I said no way was I payin' for that, and I went home and popped 'em myself.

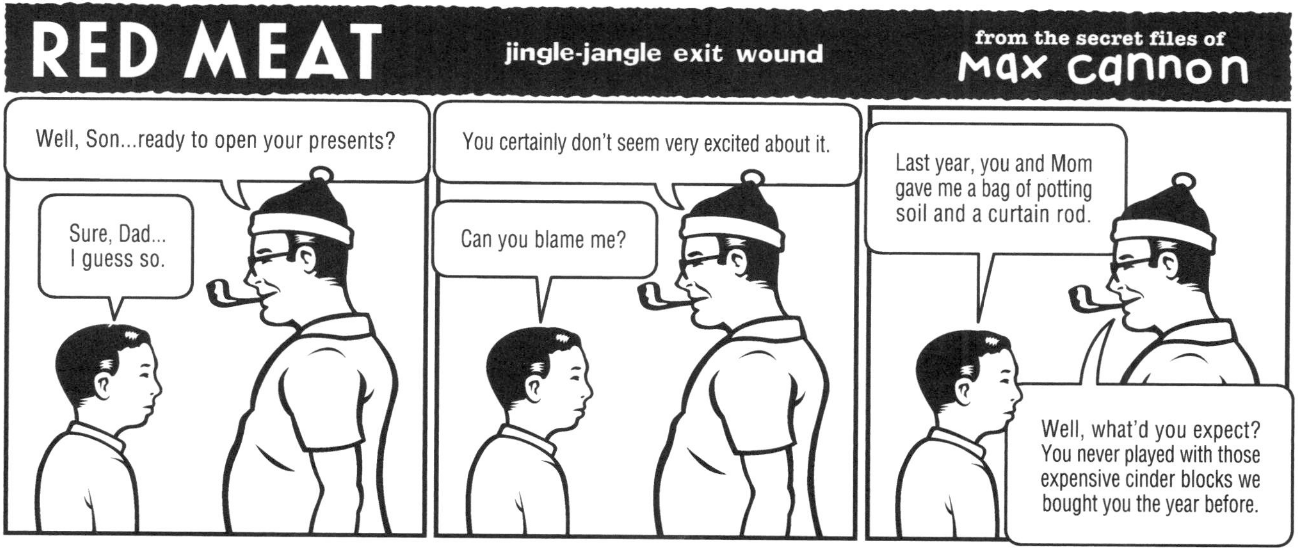
RED MEAT
jingle-jangle exit wound
from the secret files of
Max Cannon
Well, Son...ready to open your presents?
Sure, Dad... I guess so.
You certainly don't seem very excited about it.
Can you blame me?
Last year, you and Mom gave me a bag of potting soil and a curtain rod.
Well, what'd you expect? You never played with those expensive cinder blocks we bought you the year before.

RED MEAT

firmly fastened to the milk sac of misanthropy

from the secret files of **Max Cannon**

I figured them big coffee shops downtown are making a killin' by chargin' four bucks for a drink that isn't nothin' but coffee and milk and some kind of bottled flavor syrup.

So I started sellin' my own fancy coffee drinks out of my car for only two bucks, and it was goin' pretty good for awhile.

Except now I'm thinkin' I'd better start sellin' some other flavors than Mrs. Butterworth.

RED MEAT

hopped up on what you mopped up

from the secret files of
Max Cannon

Johnny Lemonhead! You seem rather lightly dressed for such a brisk day.

It's weird, Ted...the cold weather doesn't seem to be bothering me much this week.

I guess I'm still toasty warm from the other night when your bowling team burned my house to the ground with a flamethrower.

Sorry about that, John. My new teammates aren't as experienced at huffing duct sealant as I am, so they tend to get rambunctious.

RED MEAT

spring-loaded ribcage tickler

from the secret files of
Max cannon

Ahh...nothing like a movie and a bag of fresh popcorn on a Saturday afternoon. Eh, Son?

Yeah...whatever.

I remember my father used to bring me to a matinée every weekend morning.

Uh-huh.

Then he'd come back a few hours later to untie me, and take me home to lock me in the attic while he went back to the racetrack.

Now that you mention it...could you loosen the ropes just a little? My hands are numb.

So you can make a run for it? Not likely, Son.

RED MEAT

nibbled to death by marmosets

from the secret files of

Max Cannon

Okay, Johnny...ten dollars if you help me move this old trailer from the back alley to the front yard. Think you can handle it?

No problem, Ted.

So did you want to hook it up to my car or yours? I think yours might be better since my car doesn't have a trailer hitch.

Ha-ha! We won't be using a car. You'll manually pull it while I...uh, "supervise."

Gosh, Ted...That's a heavy trailer. I don't know if I'm strong enough to move it.

Nonsense. You'd be surprised at what you can do while you're being flogged.

RED MEAT

scented aspirin for perfume headaches

from the secret files of **Max Cannon**

Say, Karen...did I ever tell you about when I was in the Navy?

You were in the Navy?

Yep...but it wasn't all that great. Sometimes we were ordered to kill our own shipmates to prove our loyalty to the ranking officers.

That's a lie, Milkman Dan! My Uncle Bo is in the Navy an' they don't do mean stuff like that.

I didn't say I was in the *United States* Navy, Karen. Hmm...now that I think of it, I'm not even sure it was a navy. Is there a navy that sells kids to pirates in exchange for opium?

Mom!!

Ha-ha!! Relax...no military would ever take me. With my record, I'd be lucky to get a trout fishing license.

RED MEAT
tornado trailer park makeover
from the secret files of
Max cannon
Sir, I have a complaint I wish to file.
Look, Dan...I'm really busy. Fill out a form and leave it in my box.
Dan
But, Sir...someone has been pasting nude polaroids of me all over the walls of the employee break room. I demand that the culprit be caught and reprimanded at once.
Knock it off. I saw you gluing those photos to the wall this morning.
Dan
Wait a minute, let me get this straight... are you accusing me of posting that smut?
All the photographs have your web site's address stamped across the top.
So...you're not the least bit curious to pay a small online fee to see Milkman Dan doing more than just "posing"?

RED MEAT
poorly drawn by billy, age 8
from the secret files of
Max cannon
honney, have you seen My car keyes?
no ted.
I hadd them when I took The kids to the Lake.
did You LeFT The KeYes in The car?
mayBee, but IM noT swiming to The BoToM of the Lake to find out.

RED MEAT jackhammered funnybone powder from the secret files of **Max Cannon**

Hey, Nick. I see you're still smoking those cigarettes. Couldn't quit, huh?

What're you yapping about? I quit smoking two years ago.

Then why are you...

Wait a minute...is that a finger?

Yeah. Found it stuck in the bandsaw at work. Lotsa good marrow in these things if you chew off the bone tip.

65

RED MEAT
fully-accredited crap dojo
from the secret files of
Max Cannon
My girlfriend is always sayin' how it gives her the creeps because I sleep with my eyes open.
I don't like it neither, but I can't help it that I got this thyroid condition where I can't close my eyes. They're red and sore every mornin'.
Especially with them dang little mosquitos goin' at 'em all night.

RED MEAT
carelessly flung mud puppy chum
from the secret files of
Max Cannon
Well...I'll see you in two weeks, Son. I wish I could stay here with you at summer camp.
No you don't.
Sure I do. Who wouldn't want to wake up every morning in the great outdoors, and spend the day basking in nature's glory?
Sounds great.
Except all we did last year was scrape rust off hunks of scrap metal ten hours a day. At night, we stood next to the chain link fence watching the older kids smoke cigarettes.
Stay away from the fence, Son. The sharpshooters in these towers can pick a fly off a wall at seventy yards.

RED MEAT
mating meal of the mantid
from the secret files of
Max Cannon
As you can see from the chart, our first and second quarter earnings are down 43% over last year. I've studied the numbers carefully.
What do you propose?
In the short term, my recommendation is that we immediately liquidate most of our inventory, lay off all low-level employees and torch both the office and warehouse.
Good thinking, Johnson. What about middle management?
They'll be incarcerated in subterranean holding tanks until we can destroy all company files and shipping manifests.
Let's get started. Wait...that chart is upside down.
Well then, we're up 43%. I'll notify the sales staff that they won't be needed as hostages.

RED MEAT
rutilant rugburn raspberries
from the secret files of
Max Cannon
I been workin' on one of them public library free computers all week long, puttin' together my brand new web site for hamster lovers.
It was pretty easy.
Gettin' all them hamsters into them teensy little corsets was another thing altogether.

RED MEAT

trouser mite pleat infestation

from the secret files of
Max Cannon

Are you just going to sit in that tub and sulk?

Sorry...I can't hear you, Dear.

Stop it, Ted...you're being a baby. You can go ahead and spend the entire night in there if you want, because I'm not going to say it.

Fine. I'll sleep here.

Oh, all right. "Help...save me, Aquaman."

By Neptune...a mermaid in trouble! No time to put on my aquapants!

RED MEAT
suction-pump laugh vacuum
from the secret files of
max cannon
Do I dare even ask what you're doing on the floor there, Ted?
Just doing my exercises, Sweetheart.
Isn't that kind of hard to do with that pan of water under your hips?
I'm just following your videotape.
But that's my old "Methods of Natural Childbirthing" tape you're watching.
Oops. Better stand back then, Honey.

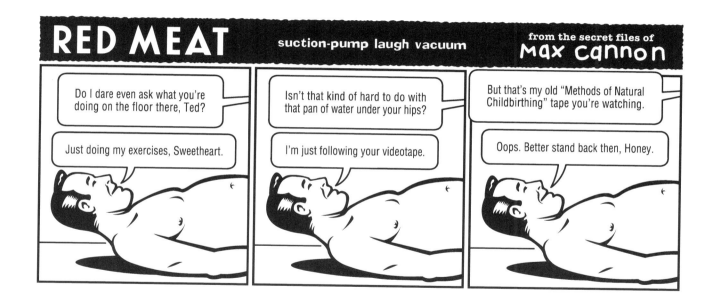

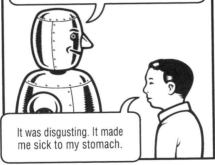

RED MEAT
inspected by number twelve
from the secret files of
max cannon
How did you enjoy the liver and tripe paté I made for your lunch yesterday?
It was disgusting. It made me sick to my stomach.
Hmm...your palette is not as refined as I had hoped. Perhaps I'd better stick to the basics.
That'd be great. Maybe plain old peanut butter and jelly.
Not that basic. I was thinking more along the lines of a classic jaw-marrow croquette.
Yuck! I'll make my own lunch, Mr. Bix.
I don't understand it. Your dog seems to love my recipes from the Gray's Anatomy cookbook.

RED MEAT

exfoliated by piranhas

from the secret files of
Max cannon

You sure are chipper today, Dan. What's the occasion?

Why does one need a special occasion to bask in the warm sunshine and drink in the sweet, clean air of a glorious day?

Well, since you put it that way...I guess you don't.

Of course, I must admit...this new high-fiber diet has been keeping me bracingly regular.

Ah. That explains why you're in my bathroom.

Nope, just borrowing a Q-tip. Better keep the kids out of the tree house for awhile, though.

73

RED MEAT
autopsy-turvy
from the secret files of
Max Cannon
Holy cow, Ken...you don't look so good today. Maybe you shouldn't be at work.
No big deal, Ted. I just have a fierce case of the Hong Kong shingles that I must've caught from one of my kids.
I'm not feeling so good myself. The kids picked up that red monkey fever at school and now my back's covered with blisters.
Ouch.
Those darned kids and their cute little diseases.
Ha! Ha! Remember back in third grade when we gave our parents lice-borne typhus?

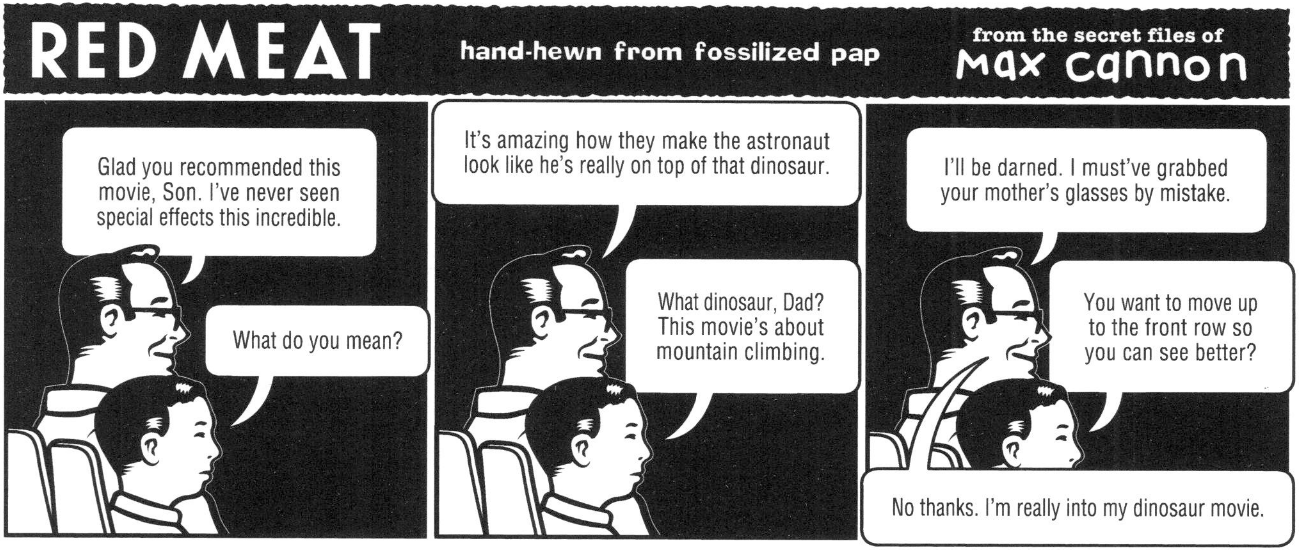

RED MEAT
hand-hewn from fossilized pap
from the secret files of
Max Cannon
Glad you recommended this movie, Son. I've never seen special effects this incredible.
What do you mean?
It's amazing how they make the astronaut look like he's really on top of that dinosaur.
What dinosaur, Dad? This movie's about mountain climbing.
I'll be darned. I must've grabbed your mother's glasses by mistake.
You want to move up to the front row so you can see better?
No thanks. I'm really into my dinosaur movie.

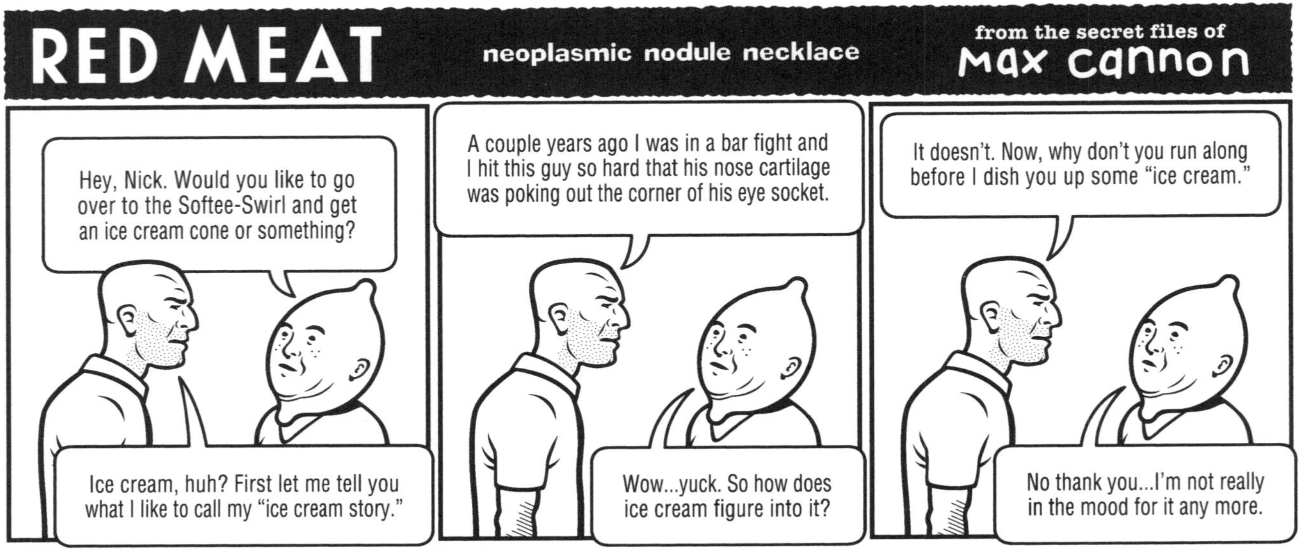

RED MEAT
neoplasmic nodule necklace
from the secret files of
Max Cannon
Hey, Nick. Would you like to go over to the Softee-Swirl and get an ice cream cone or something?
Ice cream, huh? First let me tell you what I like to call my "ice cream story."
A couple years ago I was in a bar fight and I hit this guy so hard that his nose cartilage was poking out the corner of his eye socket.
Wow...yuck. So how does ice cream figure into it?
It doesn't. Now, why don't you run along before I dish you up some "ice cream."
No thank you...I'm not really in the mood for it any more.

RED MEAT
bench-tooled laugh leather
from the secret files of
max cannon
Well...I'm here to pick you up, Son. So how was adventure camp this year?
It sucked, Dad.
The lake was infested with piranhas and they ate my new friend, Jimmy.
That's too bad, but I'll bet you made some other new friends.
Jimmy and I were the only kids here. Nobody else's parents were dumb enough to send a kid to someplace called "Camp Piranha Lake."
Take it easy there, Son. You were the one who didn't want to go back to Camp Rabid Bear Canyon this summer.

RED MEAT
leaky humorous waste containment cannister
from the secret files of
max cannon
Hon...I was thinking of making some sugar cookies. Where do you keep the baking pans?
Wouldn't it be easier if I just came down there and showed you where they are?
Ha! Nice try, Sweetheart.
No...you'll just start baking those repulsive coconut wreaths that I can't stand. I'm afraid I'll have to keep you locked in the attic for my own protection until the holidays are over.
Hey, Dad...I hate those things, too. Can you let me out of the basement?
So you can eat all my beautiful sugar cookies? Not likely, Son.

RED MEAT

the tumescent teat of torpor

from the secret files of
Max Cannon

Ted...what are you doing up at this hour? Oh my god, what happened to your hair?

I'm tired of living a lie. I've been wearing a hairpiece for years.

But I would've understood, Dear. Why didn't you tell me sooner?

I couldn't, Honey. You see...I'm a member of the "Hair Club For Men."

And the first requirement of "club membership" is that you take a lifetime oath of absolute silence.

So...I guess this means you're quitting the club?

I don't think you understand what kind of people these are, Sweetheart. You and I are going to have to "disappear" for a while. Just pack what you need, and please hurry.

79

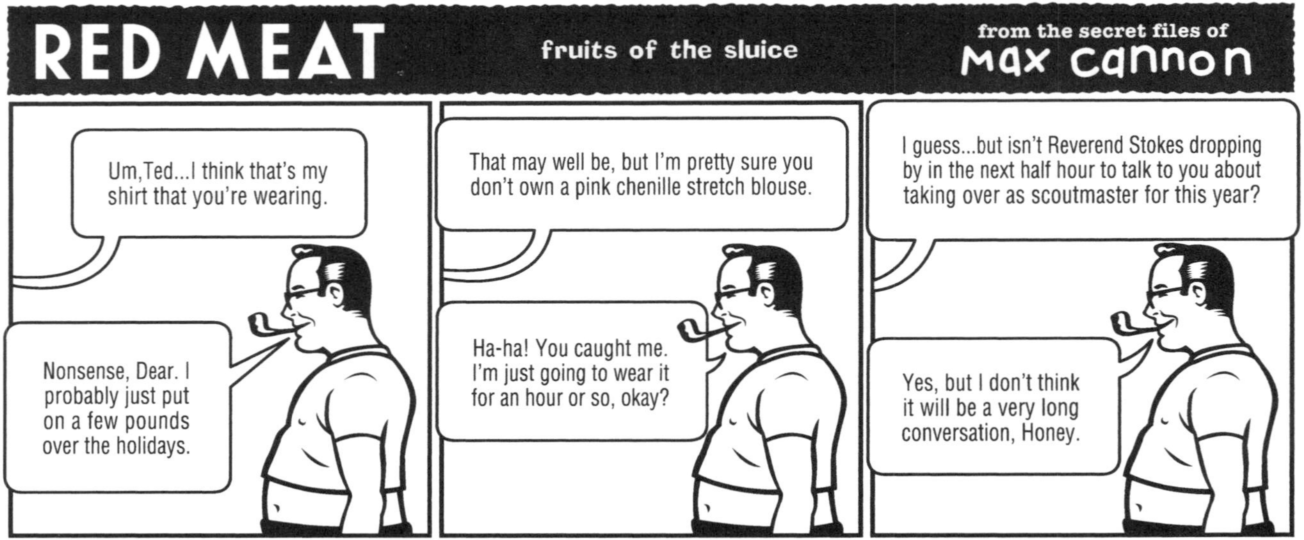
RED MEAT
fruits of the sluice
from the secret files of
Max Cannon
Um,Ted...I think that's my shirt that you're wearing.
Nonsense, Dear. I probably just put on a few pounds over the holidays.
That may well be, but I'm pretty sure you don't own a pink chenille stretch blouse.
Ha-ha! You caught me. I'm just going to wear it for an hour or so, okay?
I guess...but isn't Reverend Stokes dropping by in the next half hour to talk to you about taking over as scoutmaster for this year?
Yes, but I don't think it will be a very long conversation, Honey.

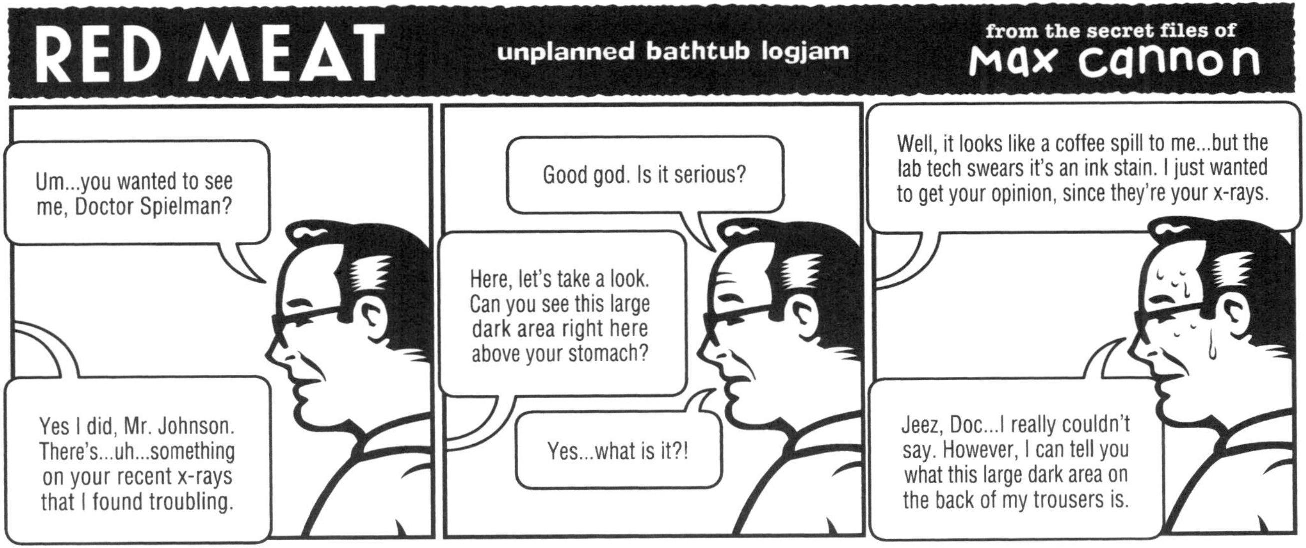
RED MEAT
unplanned bathtub logjam
from the secret files of
max cannon
Um...you wanted to see me, Doctor Spielman?
Yes I did, Mr. Johnson. There's...uh...something on your recent x-rays that I found troubling.
Good god. Is it serious?
Here, let's take a look. Can you see this large dark area right here above your stomach?
Yes...what is it?!
Well, it looks like a coffee spill to me...but the lab tech swears it's an ink stain. I just wanted to get your opinion, since they're your x-rays.
Jeez, Doc...I really couldn't say. However, I can tell you what this large dark area on the back of my trousers is.

RED MEAT
glistening spleen in the soup tureen
from the secret files of
Max Cannon
Last summer I went on a camping trip down to Mexico and I got this bad fever. I prob'ly would'a died, but this nice lady came and took care of me at my campsite.
She fed me fruit and sang me these weird songs the whole time. I thought she must be an angel, except she kept stabbin' me whenever I tried to get up for some water.
The more I think about it now...I'm pretty sure that lady was a cactus.

RED MEAT
dainty doo-dads for the despondent
from the secret files of
Max Cannon
Jeez, Nick...this heat wave is getting pretty unbearable. How can you be out jogging?
How could I not? This is prime exercise weather.
Plus, I get the opportunity to kick around wearing next-to-nothing without the usual public whining about my showin' off skin.
Right...but by "next-to-nothing," most people don't mean only a pair of running shoes, Nick.
Well, I had a sock, too. But it must've fallen off during my windsprint through the park.

RED MEAT
trilobite tracks on your teleological treatise
from the secret files of max cannon
Heavenly Father...guide me as I lead your flock toward redemption, and away from the flames of eternal damnation.
Whoa, there. "Hell" is something you made up. The way I designed it, you've just got to keep coming back until you get it right.
If it's all the same to you Lord, we're sticking with the Hell thing. It's really been working for us, so we'd prefer it if you'd just sit there and look majestic and keep that kind of thing to yourself.

RED MEAT   four flopping flats on your funmobile   from the secret files of **Max Cannon**

Panel 1:
Approach, human. You seek advice from the wise and mighty Papa Moai?

Not really. I was just wondering why you're sitting in my bushes.

Panel 2:
I have come because you spoke my name aloud, and woke me from my timeless slumber in the realm of mist.

You're mistaken, big fella. I've never even heard of you before.

Panel 3:
Wait a sec...I did just tell my wife I was going to go "pop an Old Milwaukee."

Okay, I knew that. But it sounded pretty close, and since the realm of mist doesn't have any bathrooms, I'll do anything for a "potty break."

RED MEAT
let's be honest...my kid draws like crap
from the secret files of
Max Cannon
WeL, son are you reddy to go To the store?
what?
I Thoght we were going to The Movies.
So did I. Then I remembred They dont SeLL wiskey aT movies.

RED MEAT

bulbous benzine bubblegum blisters

from the secret files of
Max Cannon

Pardon me, milk-human. Have you seen the mortal known as Ted Johnson?

Nope. If I do see him though, who should I say is looking for him?

Tell him that the wise and mighty Papa Moai wishes to transport him across many dimensions to the legendary Realm of Mist.

Sure. If I see him, I'll let him know.

Say...how would you like to pay a visit to my "Realm of Mist," friend?

If you're thinking about pushing me into those sprinklers there, you can forget it. Some kids already tried that on me earlier.

RED MEAT
pointy papules for the populace
from the secret files of
Max Cannon
Hey, Ted...guess what I just had for lunch.
I don't know, Wally...you have to give me some sort of hint.
BE-E-E-E-E-L-L-LCH!!
GAG Well, since no corpses have turned up missing, I'd have to guess that you finally ate that venison I gave you four years ago.
Yup. At least now I'll never have to wonder what a mummy tastes like.

RED MEAT
salivary stock for septic stew
from the secret files of
Max Cannon
Hey, Matt...glad I caught you. I haven't been getting my subscription of "Panel & Veneer World" magazine for the last few months, so I called the publisher and they told me they've been mailing it out.
So what makes you think I know anything about it?
For starters, I couldn't help but notice those handsome faux-woodgrain knee socks that you've been wearing lately.
You got me, Johnson...I have a problem. How about I give your magazines back to you and we pretend this never happened?
It's a deal. Say...if you'd like, I have some pretty explicit "how-to" Danish cabinetry videos that you can borrow.

RED MEAT
beetle bits in your bran flakes
from the secret files of
max cannon
'Scuse me, buddy. Wouldja mind movin' over a piece? Say, about ten foot or so?
Zzzz...what?! Who dares wake the mighty Papa Moai from his afternoon slumber?
Sorry, guy. I'm just tryin' ta do some yard workin' here, and you're standin' right in my fertilizer heap.
Oh...waitaminnit. There's my fertilizer over yonder by th' fence. How's that?
Oh, I see. Well, you're one heckuva of a deep sleeper now, ain'tcha?
Not really. I just need to quit eating so many figs before my afternoon slumber.

RED MEAT 2102

tedious tales of tomorrow

from the futuristic files of Max Cannon

Greetings, K-REN...I was hoping I'd run into you today. I just had this amazing new cyberoptic lens installed to replace my old, worn-out organic eye. How do you like it?

It looks kind of creepy. Can you see better now?

Funny you should ask that. This incredible marvel of technology enables me to clearly view a microscopic grain of pollen on the wing of bird from one hundred yards away.

Wow.

Yet, somehow I still managed to drunkenly land my hover van directly on top of your puppy's newest clone. Kind of ironic...eh?

I hate you, Genetically-Modified Soy Beverage Distribution Man Dan.

RED MEAT
peanuts on the poop deck
from the secret files of
Max Cannon
I was just thinking, Honey...how would you like to try something new tonight?
It depends, Ted. What do you have in mind?
Well, it occurred to me that in twelve years of marriage we've never given each other a spanking. Who knows...? It might be fun.
I suppose we could. I'm just afraid that I'll feel awfully silly.
Great! So...seeing as you'll already be feeling silly, it shouldn't matter if you're wearing a hand puppet while you paddle me senseless.
Can I make him talk in a pirate voice?
Aye-aye, Cap'n. I'll go get his eyepatch.

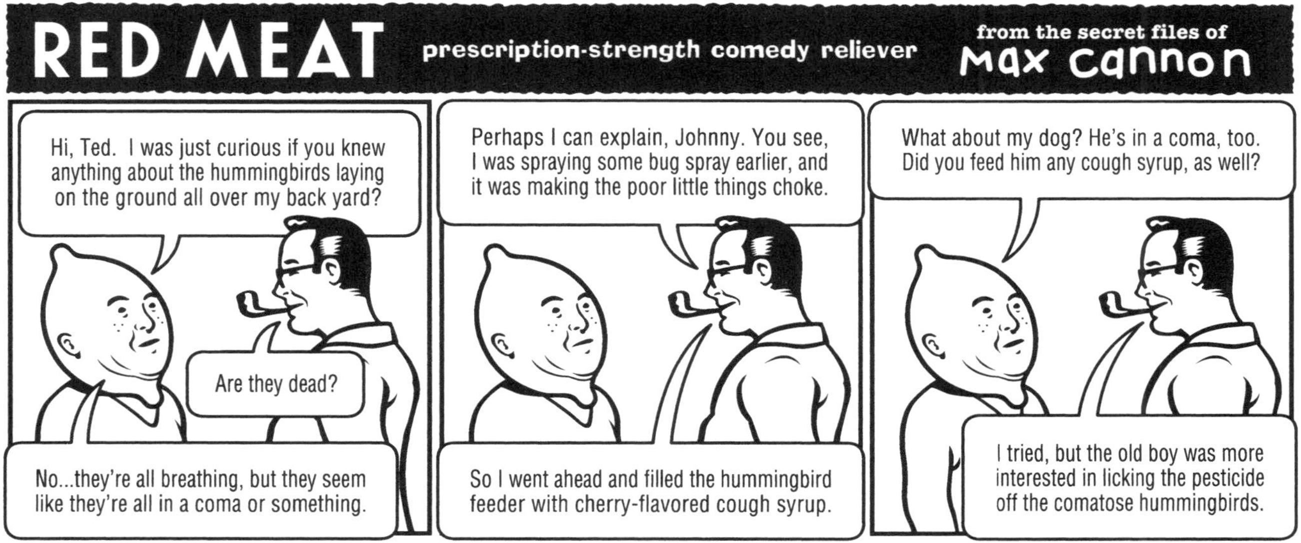

RED MEAT
prescription-strength comedy reliever
from the secret files of
Max Cannon
Hi, Ted. I was just curious if you knew anything about the hummingbirds laying on the ground all over my back yard?
Are they dead?
No...they're all breathing, but they seem like they're all in a coma or something.
Perhaps I can explain, Johnny. You see, I was spraying some bug spray earlier, and it was making the poor little things choke.
So I went ahead and filled the hummingbird feeder with cherry-flavored cough syrup.
What about my dog? He's in a coma, too. Did you feed him any cough syrup, as well?
I tried, but the old boy was more interested in licking the pesticide off the comatose hummingbirds.

RED MEAT
the pine-stench of jingle rot
from the secret files of
max cannon
Ahhh...nothing like the comforting glow of colorful twinkling lights to put you in that jolly holiday mood.
Sure, Dad...but the crackling noise kind of ruins the effect.
Yes it does, so why don't you two stop throwing rice pilaf into the bug zapper?
Sorry, Dear...but what do you expect when you put food on our holiday table that looks like assorted insect parts? Your throw, Son.

RED MEAT
headfirst into the hobart
from the secret files of
Max Cannon
I had me a couple'a rotten teeth taken out yesterday.
Now, I ain't sayin' that it didn't need to be done.
I just wish it'd been done by a dentist instead of by the bus seat in front of me.

RED MEAT
miasmic molasses for the masses
from the secret files of
max cannon
Darn it. I hate it when I wake up at five in the morning. There's nothing exciting to do until everyone else gets out of bed.
PAMPFF!!
Ahh...unless you count the indescribably sublime anticipation of waiting for an apricot to explode in the microwave oven.

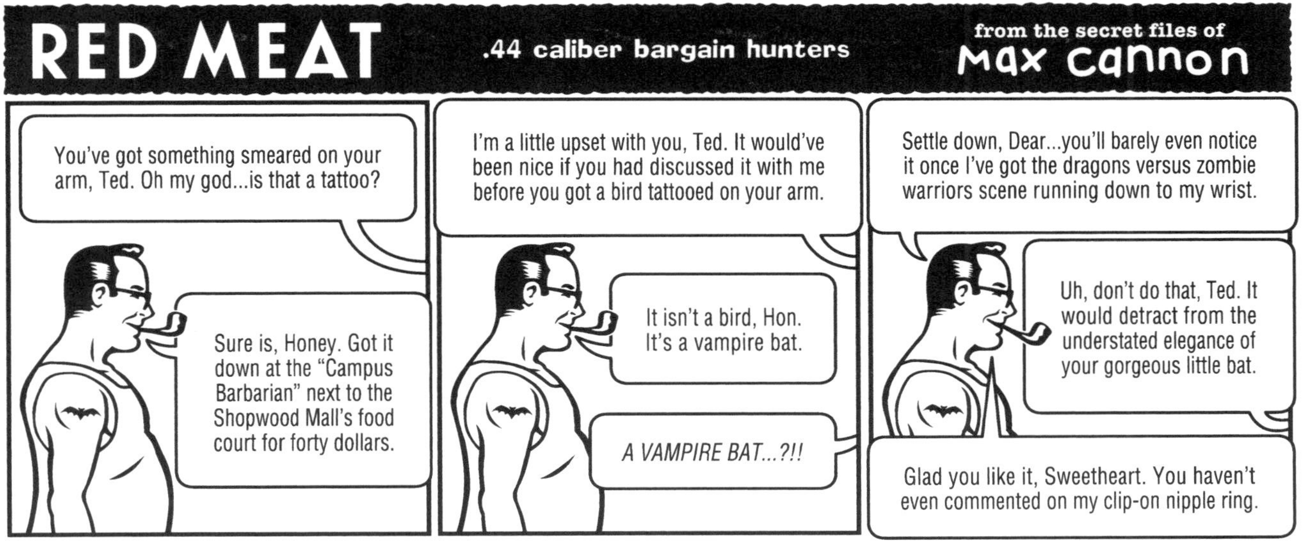

RED MEAT

.44 caliber bargain hunters

from the secret files of
Max Cannon

You've got something smeared on your arm, Ted. Oh my god...is that a tattoo?

Sure is, Honey. Got it down at the "Campus Barbarian" next to the Shopwood Mall's food court for forty dollars.

I'm a little upset with you, Ted. It would've been nice if you had discussed it with me before you got a bird tattooed on your arm.

It isn't a bird, Hon. It's a vampire bat.

A VAMPIRE BAT...?!!

Settle down, Dear...you'll barely even notice it once I've got the dragons versus zombie warriors scene running down to my wrist.

Uh, don't do that, Ted. It would detract from the understated elegance of your gorgeous little bat.

Glad you like it, Sweetheart. You haven't even commented on my clip-on nipple ring.

RED MEAT
glittering saliva chinstrap
from the secret files of
Max Cannon
Wow...that was a good one. It left a stupendous glowing red and gold trail as it streaked past.
Yeah...nice.
Sounds like you two are really enjoying that meteor shower.
We probably would be, Hon...if we hadn't gotten the inspiration to mist a couple jars full of luna moths with kerosene and turn them loose after lighting the tiki torches.
We should go grab the umbrella, Dad. They're starting to explode.

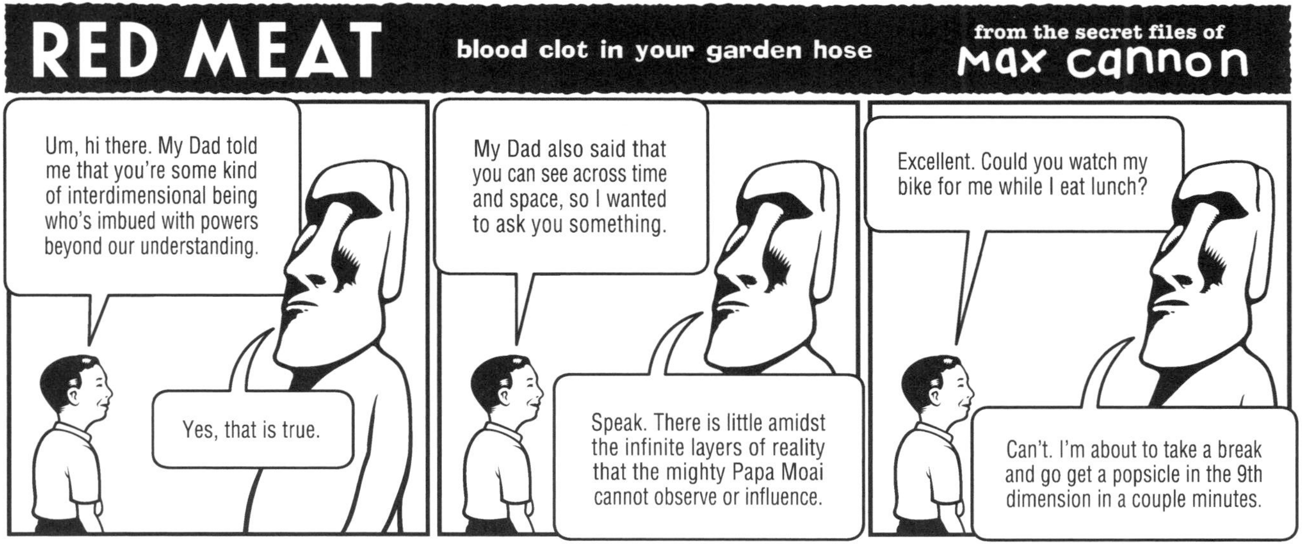
RED MEAT
blood clot in your garden hose
from the secret files of
Max Cannon
Um, hi there. My Dad told me that you're some kind of interdimensional being who's imbued with powers beyond our understanding.
Yes, that is true.
My Dad also said that you can see across time and space, so I wanted to ask you something.
Speak. There is little amidst the infinite layers of reality that the mighty Papa Moai cannot observe or influence.
Excellent. Could you watch my bike for me while I eat lunch?
Can't. I'm about to take a break and go get a popsicle in the 9th dimension in a couple minutes.

RED MEAT
who's complaining? I only paid the kid a quarter to draw this strip
from the secret files of
max cannon
Ted we have to be at diner iN ten minnuTs. you beter shavve.
but I shavved this morning.
WeL your chin is sTiLL STubeLY.
ThaTs not stubeL honny, its iron fiLings. I'm sukking on a MagneT.

RED MEAT
tarnished brass laugh snuffer
from the secret files of
Max Cannon
Look at you, Nick...you're a mess. I thought you weren't going to get in any more fights.
Relax, it wasn't a fight.
Sorry, I didn't mean to doubt you. So...were you in a car accident?
Ha! I wish. Look, when you eat as much greasy, starchy cafeteria food as I do, things are bound to get a little rough in the twice-a-month elimination process.
Now, if you'll excuse me, I better go lay down...I think I snapped my pelvis.

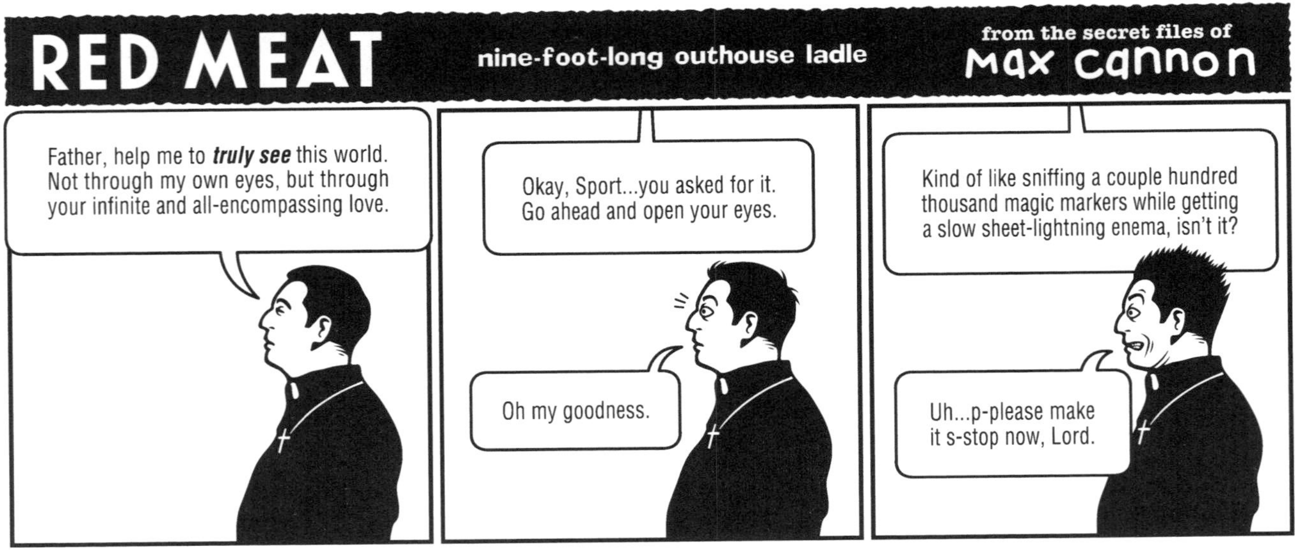
RED MEAT
nine-foot-long outhouse ladle
from the secret files of
Max Cannon
Father, help me to ***truly see*** this world. Not through my own eyes, but through your infinite and all-encompassing love.
Okay, Sport...you asked for it. Go ahead and open your eyes.
Oh my goodness.
Kind of like sniffing a couple hundred thousand magic markers while getting a slow sheet-lightning enema, isn't it?
Uh...p-please make it s-stop now, Lord.

RED MEAT
caramel bar molar removal
from the secret files of
Max Cannon
I still live...
Gaze upon me...
It can talk all it wants...I ain't gonna look.
www.I_still_live.org
Well...I s'pose it couldn't hurt nothin' to take a look at its non-profit web site.

RED MEAT
sausages in your slipstream
from the secret files of
max cannon
Good evening, Karen. Is your mom around?
Yes...why?
I'm taking her out on a dinner date tonight.
It's no secret that old Milkman Dan has had his eye on your mom for quite some time. Who knows...? Maybe this could lead to something truly magical for me.
But you're a mean jerk. I don't want my momma datin' somebody like you.
I know. That's the most magical part of all.
I hate you, Milkman Dan!
It's amazing how much that sounds like "Milkman Dad."
Shut up! Shut up!

RED MEAT
horse track flapjacks
from the secret files of
Max Cannon
Lord a'mighty...jus' this mornin' me and the boys found two'a my steer out in the arroyo 'bout a hunnert yards or so out from the corral.
Eyeballs popped clean out an' their innards all boiled inside 'em. Don't know whut t'make of it.
Hells bells, I'd almost start b'lievin' them crazy yarns 'bout outer space UFO saucers a'comin' down an' messin' with livestock.
'Course, I gotta admit we fed them cattle quite a bit of my home-brewed liquid methadrine to keep 'em dancin' at last night's hoe-down.
Boss...we found Dwight. He was out cold under one'a the steer.
Well, throw some clothes on 'im and git 'im some black coffee. We still gotta figure out how'ta git that heifer down off the water tank.

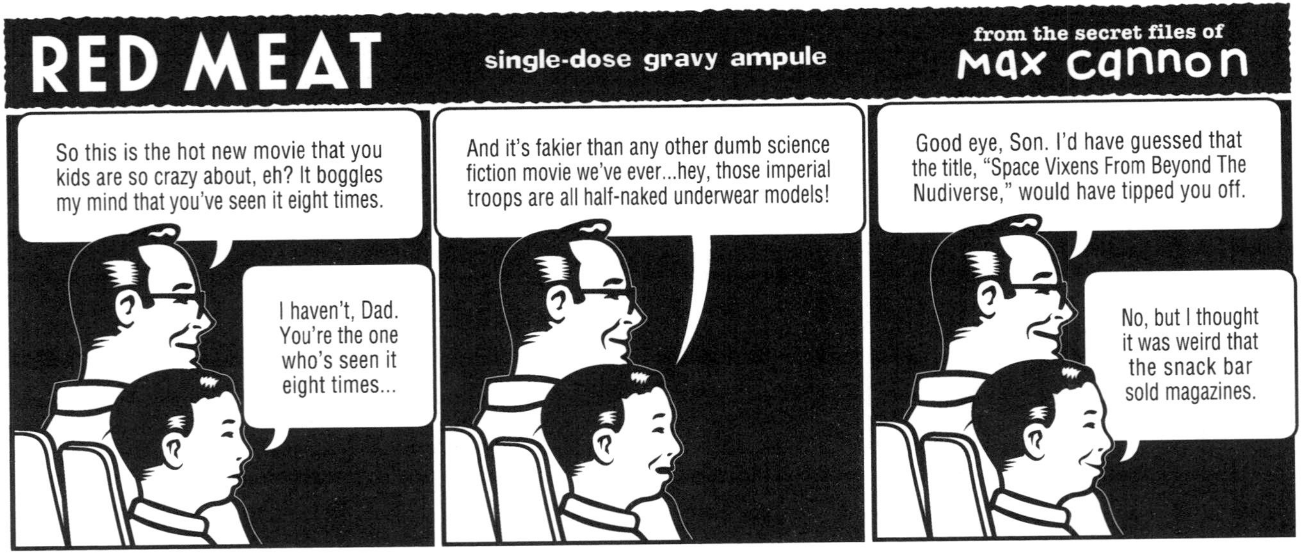
RED MEAT
single-dose gravy ampule
from the secret files of
max cannon
So this is the hot new movie that you kids are so crazy about, eh? It boggles my mind that you've seen it eight times.
I haven't, Dad. You're the one who's seen it eight times...
And it's fakier than any other dumb science fiction movie we've ever...hey, those imperial troops are all half-naked underwear models!
Good eye, Son. I'd have guessed that the title, "Space Vixens From Beyond The Nudiverse," would have tipped you off.
No, but I thought it was weird that the snack bar sold magazines.

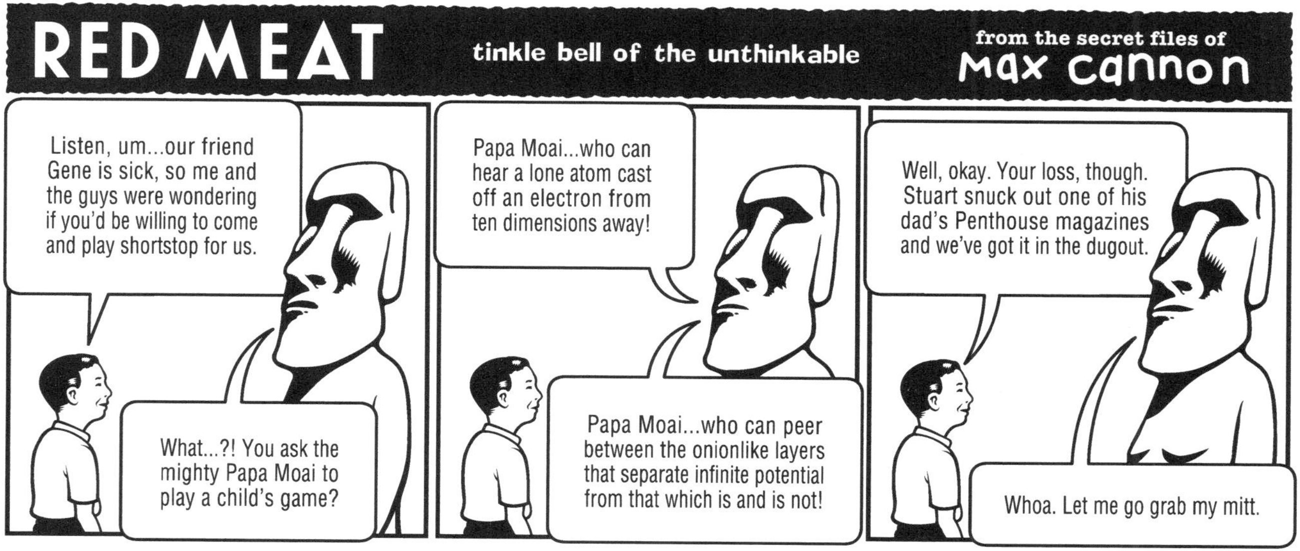
RED MEAT
tinkle bell of the unthinkable
from the secret files of
Max cannon
Listen, um...our friend Gene is sick, so me and the guys were wondering if you'd be willing to come and play shortstop for us.
What...?! You ask the mighty Papa Moai to play a child's game?
Papa Moai...who can hear a lone atom cast off an electron from ten dimensions away!
Papa Moai...who can peer between the onionlike layers that separate infinite potential from that which is and is not!
Well, okay. Your loss, though. Stuart snuck out one of his dad's Penthouse magazines and we've got it in the dugout.
Whoa. Let me go grab my mitt.

RED MEAT
virulent laugh pathogen
from the secret files of
max cannon
It's over 90°, Ted...and you're wearing that outfit to do yard work? I thought you got rid of that body fluid harvesting suit last summer after drinking from it made you ill.
I modified it, Honey. Now the harvested sweat and excretions are triple-filtered.
So now it doesn't make you sick to your stomach when you drink the recycled fluid?
Uh, I wouldn't make that claim, exactly.
That's why I added a high-speed fermentation unit, so at least now I'm roaring drunk while I chug my own foul, musky, repulsive juices.
So...what's with the chest spigot?
I call it the "honey spout," to share my intoxicating man-nectar with others.

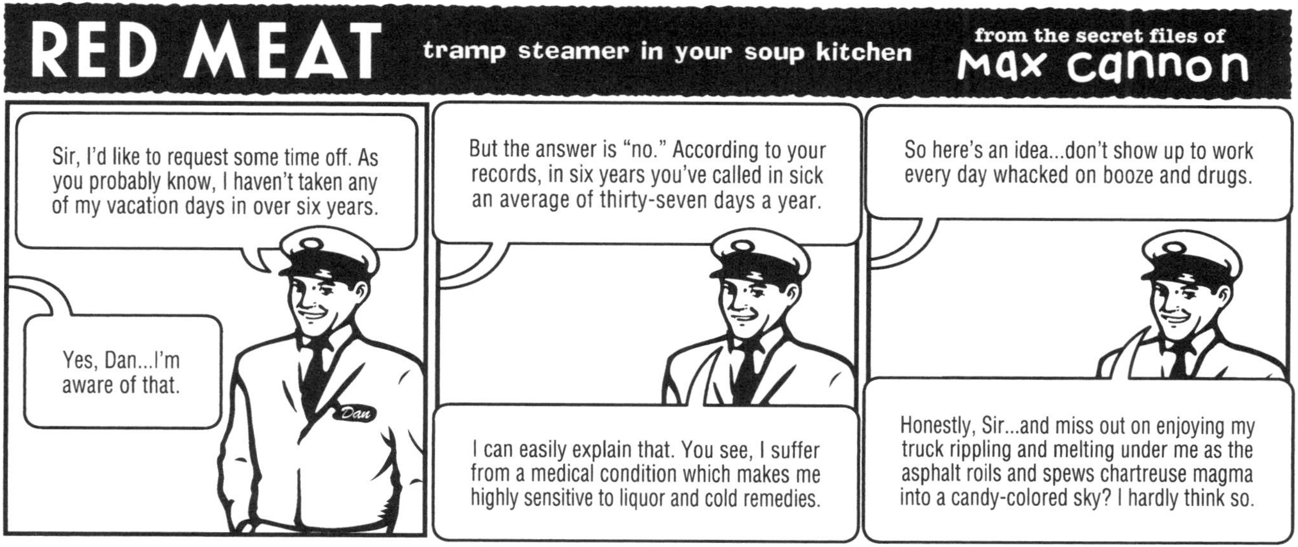
RED MEAT
tramp steamer in your soup kitchen
from the secret files of
max cannon
Sir, I'd like to request some time off. As you probably know, I haven't taken any of my vacation days in over six years.
Yes, Dan...I'm aware of that.
Dan
But the answer is "no." According to your records, in six years you've called in sick an average of thirty-seven days a year.
I can easily explain that. You see, I suffer from a medical condition which makes me highly sensitive to liquor and cold remedies.
So here's an idea...don't show up to work every day whacked on booze and drugs.
Honestly, Sir...and miss out on enjoying my truck rippling and melting under me as the asphalt roils and spews chartreuse magma into a candy-colored sky? I hardly think so.

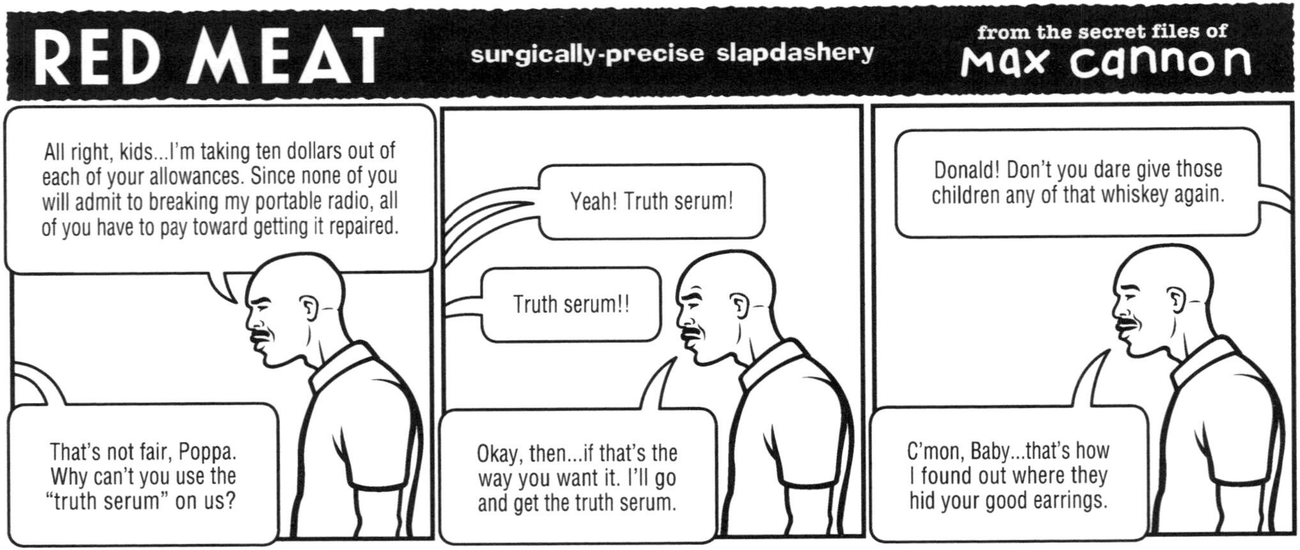
RED MEAT
surgically-precise slapdashery
from the secret files of
max cannon
All right, kids...I'm taking ten dollars out of each of your allowances. Since none of you will admit to breaking my portable radio, all of you have to pay toward getting it repaired.
That's not fair, Poppa. Why can't you use the "truth serum" on us?
Yeah! Truth serum!
Truth serum!!
Okay, then...if that's the way you want it. I'll go and get the truth serum.
Donald! Don't you dare give those children any of that whiskey again.
C'mon, Baby...that's how I found out where they hid your good earrings.

RED MEAT
hull breach in the gravy boat
from the secret files of
Max Cannon
Honestly, Ted. I paid a lot for these nice silk boxer shorts... and you won't even wear them.
Nothing personal, Honey. I just don't like the way they get all crinkled up and shiny-looking in the morning sun. It's purely an aesthetic issue for me.
Fair enough. However, would you at least consider putting some type of garment on the lower half of your body?
Not if it compromises the complex interplay of light and shadow over the rich terrain of my alabaster lap.

For more *RED MEAT* strips, news, interactive features and a unique selection of quality *RED MEAT* books and merchandise, please visit

www.redmeat.com